POEMS, ESSAYS, AND SHORT STORIES FOR SHARING

Portraits of a Writer's Soul!

Denise Michelle Phillips

POEMS, ESSAYS, AND SHORT STORIES FOR SHARING
Portraits of a Writer's Soul!

by Denise Michelle Phillips

Rhodes-Fulbright Library

ProdCode: CSS/250/4.24/232/16

Library of Congress Catalog Card Number

International Standard Book Number

1-55605-300-2

Copyright © 2000 by Denise Michelle Phillips

ALL RIGHTS RESERVED

Printed in the United States of America

Wyndham Hall Press
Bristol, IN 46507-9460

DEDICATION

This momentous occasion is to be shared with Mr. and Mrs. Richard Goodwin, friends from New York, who were the first to read my manuscript. Their laborious and time consuming endeavor, along with their warmth and sensitivity, will always be remembered and cherished.

ACKNOWLEDGMENTS

While struggling with my poetic demons, Mr. Richard Girard Martinez, a friend from Albuquerque, New Mexico, kept me focused and sane during my temporary bouts of insanity. Richard, thanks for your loving support.

Special recognition to my students in the English, Writing, and Poetry classes for invaluable feedback, patience, and understanding. The gleam in your eyes and the smiles on your faces inspired me to fight-the-good-fight!

Finally, my gratitude to Mrs. Gary Archibeck, Albuquerque, for her computer expertise. Mrs. Archibeck, you came through for me, and you're a saint in disguise!

TABLE OF CONTENTS

ACKNOWLEDGMENTS i

GOD ISN'T THROUGH WITH ME YET! 1

A TRIBUTE TO A STRONG AND POWERFUL
    BLACK MAN 3

THE BLACK MAN REVISITED: A Letter of Apology! 5

A LOVING TRIBUTE TO THE FORGOTTEN
    BLACK WOMAN IN AMERICA 7

PEOPLE WHO CAN'T BE ALONE 9

LOOKING FOR MR. RIGHT IN ALL THE
    WRONG PLACES 10

DON'T FENCE ME IN! 12

THE SAFETY NET 13

GOING DOWN MEMORY LANE: Comfort Foods of
    My Youth 14

WHY SHOULD WE BE THANKFUL? 17

A FINAL TRIBUTE TO THE KNOWN SOLDIER,
    MICHAEL BLASSIE 18

FIDDLING WITH TIME 20

MOUNTAINS OF COURAGE 21

THE WINGS OF FAITH 22

A MOTHER'S PRAYER TO HER CREATOR 23

A HYMN OF PRAISE TO MOTHER NATURE:
   A Celebration of God's Handiwork 24

LOVING TRIBUTES FROM A SON, HUSBAND,
   AND FATHER 27

A TRIBUTE TO TEACHERS 30

ARE WE TOO POLITICALLY CORRECT? 31

JUST BECAUSE OF MY SEX! 32

SWEET INNOCENCE 34

A MARTYR OF THE FAITH 35

ANGEL OF MERCY 36

THE HANGMENS' NOOSE! 37

THESE HALLOWED HALLS ON CAPITOL HILL 38

WHAT DID YOU SAY YOUR NAME WAS, AGAIN? 40

A TOUCH OF CLASS 41

IN RECOGNITION OF OUR SENIOR CITIZENS:
   Accolades Long Overdue 42

A TRIBUTE TO THE STATUE OF LIBERTY 43

THIS ENCHANTING CITY: Albuquerque, New Mexico 44

IN THE BLEAK MIDWINTER: New York City Revisited 45

SWEET, SOFT SUMMER RAIN	47
THE FLOWERS OF MY YOUTH!	48
THE GIFT OF LIFE!	49
WHEN GOD MADE WOMAN	50
THOUGHTS OF YOU	51
THE LAST TIME I SAW YOU!	52
IF I HAD TO DO IT OVER AGAIN, I'D	53
DETOUR FROM MY HEART	56
REMEMBER?	57
TIDAL BOUT	60
TRUE TO OURSELVES!	61
FRANKLY SPEAKING!	62
THOSE LONG, SUMMER NIGHTS	63
WHAT'S HAPPINESS?	64
PRICELESS TREASURE	65
REFLECTING ON THE JOYS OF CHILDHOOD	66
WHEN TIMES WERE GOOD	67
AN ACT OF KINDNESS!	69
I'M JUST A STRANGER PASSING THROUGH!	70

NOBODY LOVES ME!	71
SOMEBODY'S CHILD	73
MY ENEMIES ARE SEEKING MY SOUL!	75
BETRAYED	76
MOMMY, WHERE'S DADDY?	77
THE FARMERS' MARKET	81
A BUS CALLED ANYWHERE	82
GOD, WHAT AM I DOING HERE?	83
GOD, I'M NOT ANGRY AT YOU!	85
THIS IS YOUR LIFE!	88
LIFE'S PLAYFUL VIGNETTES	91
GENERATION X	94
WHY WON'T SOCIETY LEAVE OTHERS ALONE?	95
WHEN A HOUSE ISN'T A HOME!	96
BURNING DESIRE!	97
MISS STRUTTIN' HER STUFF!	98
ILLEGAL AND UNWANTED	100
RAINY DAY, STORMY NIGHT!	102
THE PLAYER	104

THE LADIES OF THE EVENING	105
LIVING ON THE EDGE	106
THE DEMONS WITHIN	108
THE PRISONER OF MY SOUL	109
DEADLY SILENCE	111
THE UNATTAINABLE	113
1999 AND COUNTING	114

GOD ISN'T THROUGH WITH ME YET!

I've been through some rough times, then again, who hasn't. This essay is about me, and why I'm sharing my experiences. However, God's enduring mercy extended my earthly stay a little longer because of unfinished business. Furthermore, I believe angels are watching and protecting me from dangers seen and unseen.

On Tuesday, July 14, 1998 at 2:50 a.m., someone touched me, told me to get up, and write! The poem, *A Tribute To A Strong And Powerful Black Man*, answered that call. Anyway, I wasn't too serious about writing until that memorable morning. I finally completed these colorful portraits Monday, October 12, 1998.

I didn't have difficulty being creative because the titles came to me, naturally. Nevertheless, some of the poems were quite touching: *Sweet Innocence, A Martyr Of The Faith, Angel Of Mercy,* and two of my favorites: *The Flowers Of My Youth* and *My Enemies Are Seeking My Soul!* Therefore, going in-and-out of character was emotionally draining.

The residents at the correctional facility gave me inspiration, too. As a matter of fact, I dedicated this poem to them: *God, What Am I Doing Here?* The essay, *In The Bleak Midwinter: New York City Revisited*, and the poem, *A Tribute To The Statue Of Liberty*, are personal memories because I used to live in New York and work there.

In Recognition Of Our Senior Citizens: Accolades Long Overdue was a much deserved dedication. I was admiring two senior citizens in the local park when the title for this essay came to me. It was also in that same park I heard a little girl ask her mother: "mommy, where's daddy?" That question caught my attention, and of course, you know the rest: a short story was born.

A Hymn Of Praise To Mother Nature: A Celebration Of God's Handiwork, an adoration, pays homage to God's creations. When the poetic juices flow, I'm usually walking and observing people; listening to residents in a conversation; walking through the campus appreciating nature; listening to the news; reading the newspapers; or just meditating. Notwithstanding, I had to write now, not later! On the other hand, some of you may find yourselves laughing hysterically, crying uncontrollably, or sitting impassively.

Finally, I've enjoyed writing these poetic portraits. Please share them with family, friends, and neighbors.

A TRIBUTE TO A STRONG AND POWERFUL BLACK MAN

This overdue tribute greets you with the
respect and dignity you deserve. You,
black man, with your proud, strong
shoulders bearing centuries of oppression.

The guilt, shame, fear, and hopelessness
you carry pricks at the core of my soul,
a soul searching, seeking for unknown
truths about your existence: an existence
you've labored with your blood, sweat,
and tears!

Lying here unattended by the trappings
of a husband, lover, or friend, I think of
you constantly: tossing and turning in a
cold, shameful bed. Ashamed that I've
been guilty, at one time or another, of
abandoning you in a society which
ignores your valuable talents and
contributions, but graciously accepts your
playful spirit on a basketball court as
the crowds shout: "go, go, shoot, shoot!"
"Two points -- that's my man!" The
screams of elation from fans who
knowingly use you to compensate for
their inadequacies infuriates me. I
dare not wrestle with the dark secrets
of my heart: these little hells consuming
and engulfing me like a fireball within the
furnace of my soul! For so long, I've
been emotionally, physically, and
spiritually absent from your presence.
Benign neglect, you call it? You're much
too kind.

I long to have your strong, dominant
powerful hips trapped between my weak,
troubled thighs as I await your grand
entry: moaning, groaning, inhaling, and
exhaling with quivering lips, anticipating
your seed for the fatal thrust into the pit
of my pleasure! Yes, that's it; right there.
Then again, why should I doubt your
masculinity? You never miss your target!

This is for real. Do you doubt me? Your
black, unassuming woman accepts your
pain of rejection as you ejaculate centuries
of oppression and explore my vastness!
No doubt, I joyfully receive this gift from
such a welcomed guest.

As we lie speechless, we stare
innocently into each other's eyes
for words. There are no words
expressing our love. Then, fading
away into a light slumber and
jolting from a throbbing, orgasmic
experience, I scream: "two points!"

THE BLACK MAN REVISITED: A Letter of Apology!

My black man,

This letter is true from my heart because you don't possess physical, powerful attributes, only. You're much more than a sexual acrobat! What I failed to come across in *A Tribute To A Strong And Powerful Black Man* is your rich ancestry: renowned and respected with proven track records leading to your past and present successes.

You know your deadlines, and you don't miss them. No one has to tell you what to do and when to do it. You take care of business by taking advantage of available opportunities. Your successes and failures are dependent upon appropriate strategic planning. Planning affected your choosing historical black colleges. Believe me, there wasn't anything wrong with selecting other ones.

You're aware many of your ancestors ate, studied, laughed, cried, dated, and graduated from these fine institutions. Please don't develop amnesia after pursuing your goals. Someone made emotional and financial sacrifices for you. In retrospect, don't forget "the bridge" that carried you across: the kindness of a stranger, a church's support, or your family. While stumbling trying to recover, someone, somewhere was praying for you!

Remember, the established black colleges should be recognized -- and not spoken in hushed, embarrassed tones, but loudly proclaimed and celebrated. These institutions reflect your rich culture.

Now, for the successful black men who didn't attend college, I salute you for your pioneering spirit and tenacity in overcoming obstacles. I'm sure your road wasn't paved with gold as you walked rough pavements, climbed high mountains, and cried countless tears. Your abiding faith in God and your family sustained you through rough times, and by the way, your faith is still sustaining you.

Never, never give up on your dreams because when you stop dreaming, you die! The road to success isn't easy, and God didn't promise you a rose garden. He promised He wouldn't leave you or forsake you. So, if He's not willing to forsake you, you owe it to yourself not to renege on your promise to be the best that you can be!

Finally, always value yourself and don't let others label you. You're a fighter, not a loser! Keep the faith and take the Lord with you -- everywhere you go.

A LOVING TRIBUTE TO THE FORGOTTEN BLACK WOMAN IN AMERICA

Black woman, you've been feared, loved, hated, abused, accused, and misunderstood! You're still being avoided by some who are afraid of knowing you. There are the fearful who would rather prejudge you on the basis of your sex or color.

You're undaunted by life's temporary setbacks because of rough, troubling waters: swimming and keeping your head above water because you're too proud to drown! You'll not give your attackers the benefit of your death: while resting on the shores of time before regaining and recovering your strength.

Your shoulders are the bearer of heavy burdens, and it's amazing you're maintaining your balance! Lord knows, you're weary and rightly so. There are some who are afraid of carrying your cross because of stereotypes, ignorance, misconceptions, defiance, or immaturity. Even though you've a mind of your own, you can't be controlled.

Quite frankly, family is important. The media are sometimes misinterpreting your cue card. Whether you're single; separated; married; divorced; widowed; or living with a partner, it doesn't matter. Labels aren't important because having self-worth is crucial for your survival.

Your expression speaks volumes of truths without you uttering a sound! Your physique is a sculptured work of art endowed by your Creator. You've absolutely nothing to hide and shame shouldn't be in your expansive vocabulary. You're molded for greatness because people envy your persistence in the face of challenges.

Anticipating the new century, you're packed and ready for sailing. There are many places to go and adventures to seek. Remember, you're always attempting to do your best: striving for excellence and not mediocrity.

You don't want defining by television, magazines, newspaper editorials, or other's perceptions. Your rich legacy is defined because it's etched in time. Your dreams are only set by your limitations, not by others. Once successful, don't forget those who shared significant roles in your achievement. They were truly your Rock of Gibraltar: strong, nurturing pillars in the community who cried when you cried and laughed when you laughed. They were also singing their praises of Zion in the Wednesday night prayer services while you were at study hall.

Finally, don't forget prayer changes things. Always ask God's guidance before seeking your endeavors. When you're richly blessed, don't forget to give Him the praise and the glory!

PEOPLE WHO CAN'T BE ALONE

I know too many people who can't be alone, or should I say, refuse to be alone. If it's a warm body, they'll accept anyone in their lives. If you ask them why they chose that person, their usual response is "a piece of man/woman is better than no one at all!"

What's wrong with that picture? Doesn't that thinking sound a little distorted? There isn't anything wrong with having a healthy (sane), meaningful, and reciprocal relationship. The problem lies in settling for someone and using them until discovering "the" significant other.

Most people refusing to be alone are usually insecure, possessing low or no self-esteem, and are too dependent on others. There's no sin in being alone, if it's your choice. Often, most people need introspection before entering relationships. For some, they're too impatient and impulsive. Their mind is on having someone today at any cost because tomorrow's not promised.

Learning to love yourself can be very difficult and challenging for some people since they weren't shown love in their formative years. However, you can't love anyone until you love yourself because your relationships will suffer. Why put your significant other through those changes? Honesty is important! If you're not ready for a relationship, tell your lover. It's better he/she finds out now rather than later because that kind of dishonesty can sometimes backfire with severe consequences!

Most importantly, be good to yourself whether or not you have a special someone in your life. People normally don't respect those who are abusive to themselves. Avoid people who are detrimental to your character and your sense of well being: emotionally, morally, and spiritually.

LOOKING FOR MR. RIGHT IN ALL THE WRONG PLACES

Now, this advice is for you ladies who spend your salary on fancy wardrobes and accessories to attract your Mr. Right! Are some of you sitting by the phone hoping he'll call? Do you get the urge to call? Would he consider you aggressive, too pushy if you took the initiative to call? (Pray, he's a liberated man of the 90s and beyond!) If you haven't noticed, the social taboos are lifted. You can be free being who you are, and of course, facing the consequences of your choices!

Which brings me to the point. Why are you looking for Mr. Right in all the wrong places? Where do you say you go looking: bars; social clubs; perusing newspaper personals, the Internet, or for the adventurous, street cruising? I'm not suggesting you won't find a man, but girlfriend, you're looking for Mr. Right, and that's the big difference!

I knew someone who discovered her man in the meat section of her supermarket. In fact, she wasn't really looking for anyone. He just happened to be standing there when their eyes locked. That's how she found her Mr. Right!

Another friend discovered her man in the deacon's pew of her Baptist Church. Just before the service and during the devotional, he looked at her, smiling. I guess God works in mysterious ways! The last time I heard, she's a deaconess, his wife!

I've another friend, a professional photographer, who was photographing a basketball game and happened to be standing by a famous basketball player who caught her attention. I heard she scored two points herself: hooped her dream man, resulting in a Kodak moment!

My cousin's friend was at a cemetery grieving for a loved one when she noticed a handsome man standing next to her. I was told she instantly dried those tears! Well, after the graveside service, he asked her out.

Another friend is into the art scene. She was walking around, observing famous masterpieces when a human work of art walked toward her. Now, she and her art lover boyfriend are dating.

You're still not convinced there's a Mr. Right somewhere? OK, I've another cousin living in New York City, and taking the subway, a tall, handsome guy sat next to her reading his newspaper (or pretending) and started talking about the weather and his job. Well, telephone numbers were exchanged and a relationship was started. Ladies, there's someone for you if you'll only open your eyes, be prepared for the unexpected, and go for it! You might be saying to your friends: "I was looking for Mr. Right, and he was in all the right places!"

DON'T FENCE ME IN!

There are some women locked in old-fashioned traditions with boyfriends or husbands refusing any negotiations concerning the new feminism of the 90s. ["You've come a long way, baby." "It's the nineties, do your own thing," or "I've gotta be me!"] To these men, your dreams and goals vanished when you met them. These men won't hear your cries: "don't fence me in!"

Sometimes, the pressures and cares of everyday life are unbearable. There are no support systems from family, boyfriends, or husbands, but plenty of negativity and disillusionment. You know, some men lie! They don't honestly tell you their expectations when they're dating. It's the sin of omission thing!

Boyfriends, husbands -- unlock those chains binding your women. They aren't animals. (Some animals have more freedom without their leashes!) Don't inhibit their dreams leading to peace of mind, happiness, and independence from your kingly dominance.

THE SAFETY NET

I don't want to be someone's safety net.
I'm not here to catch them or be a
recipient of their volatile relationships
when they're unhappy!

Don't attach yourself like an octopus,
strangling me in your arms because
you're afraid of seeking unknown
challenges for fear of being hurt!

Don't use me for your adventurous
schemes when you're alone, but
ignoring me when you're safely secured
in your lover's arms. Weren't we friends
before you met him? Now, you've
disowned me. I know it's only temporary
until you call me crying for comfort and
solace.

One day, I'm not going to be at your
disposal to use. My listening ears will
be plugged, my hands will be extended
to others who care, and my lips will no
longer offer advice. Your safety net
will be severed, and you'll be left
dangling from its loose ends!

GOING DOWN MEMORY LANE: Comfort Foods of my Youth

Miss Mary, affectionately called, was short, plump, and vivacious. She was known for pleasant aromas coming from her large kitchen (which she had redone for the sole purpose of feeding the multitude in the community). To her, everyday was a food festival! You could be a block away and smell Miss Mary's home cooking.

God gave her a talent, and she used it above and beyond the call of duty. She'd always volunteer for the church's food committee. Miss Mary loved and respected food, and of course, it showed on her ample hips: especially sitting in her favorite white rocking chair on the airy porch, overlooking the almost saintly neighborhood. (We used to jokingly say that she could smell sin a mile away!)

Miss Mary would rock back-and-forth shelling peas, snapping beans, while singing her favorite hymns: "Blessed Assurance Jesus is Mine" and "What A Fellowship, What A Joy Divine, Leaning On The Everlasting Arms." She especially loved the refrain: leaning on the everlasting arms. Miss Mary would belt out this hymn with her husky, powerful voice! If the neighbors were passing by, they'd join in, too. She felt her music: deep, down in her soul. Since she delighted in spreading The Gospel, she wasn't one for telling you how to live, she joyfully "lived" her sermons! If she saw you on the street, she'd invite you in for a meal. God help if you were too thin. Miss Mary's hospitality was more than gracious. Her breakfasts were powerful. Have you heard the expression power breakfast? Well, I guess she coined the phrase. It wasn't unusual having sausage; bacon; ham; grits; eggs; homemade biscuits; pancakes; or waffles; hot coffee; and juice on different days. When leaving her table, you just wanted to sleep!

Her dinners were just as filling. It wasn't uncommon eating three or four home grown vegetables; always two meats; at least two starches; pan fried bread in that rich, black cast iron skillet; or homemade biscuits with butter drooling down the sides; two desserts; cold tea; or lemonade. Not eating with Miss Mary was considered rude and insensitive: eating with her was your rite of passage!

One morning, I was running errands for her, and as a token of payment, she fed me a late breakfast consisting of smothered pork chops, eggs, biscuits, grits, and gravy. While breakfast was being served, Miss Mary was cooking her dinner while it was still cool. (They didn't have air-conditioners back then.) Guess what she had? Fresh collard greens with ham hocks; fresh string beans with country ham; fried chicken; meat loaf; macaroni and cheese; cabbage; candied yams; cornbread; sweet potato pie; and peach cobbler. You know, she had her cold, mint tea and lemonade for quenching my thirst.

Today, I'm sorry to say, it's a little different. Most of the Miss Marys don't cook like that any more because their children have left home. Occasionally, you'll visit someone on a special holiday, and you can smell those aromas coming from the kitchen as you land at the airport!

Some working women today don't have the time to cook like their mothers because they're too busy earning a living. Most women in Miss Mary's generation were working domestic jobs, coming home cooking, and cleaning for their families. I think some women today are spoiled by the fast-paced food technology called take-outs. I'm not suggesting eating as if it's your last supper, but in your hurried pace: stopping, wonderfully savoring, and enjoying cooking at its finest. You don't have to wait until Thanksgiving, Christmas, or Easter for getting together and enjoying one another's company.

If you remember back then, people generally ate what they wanted and lived a long life. Oh, some might say that the vegetables were freshly grown, and there weren't many preservatives. True, people smoked and drank, but their longevity was, and still is, a mystery to me. Fortunately, we're blessed with modern appliances and other make-our-lives-easier conveniences, and some of us are still complaining about time management. If I had my choice, I'd prefer the simpler times because Miss Mary was "the" community and her spirited generosity was untouchable! In those days, families, extended families, and friends were the cornerstone of the community. Also, the preachers echoed these words: "the families that prayed together, stayed together!" Honestly, we were truly blessed having those saints around reminding us of that "Blessed Assurance." Miss Mary, thanks for the wonderful memories and rest in peace!

WHY SHOULD WE BE THANKFUL?

We've so much to be thankful
for that some aren't acknowledging
or appreciating the wonders of
creation. When we're awakening
to a sunrise, it's time for rejoicing
in the new morning!

It's time to say thank you Jesus
when we're smelling blooming
flowers while observing a colorful
butterfly in flight!

We should be echoing our praises
to the Most High when we see a
beautiful sunset, marvel at a cloud,
watch puppies play, and enjoy the
first fruits of spring!

When we're eating from the rich
bountiful harvest provided by our
Creator, we should be giving thanks!

Our gratitude should be overwhelming
in a country where there are freedom of
choices!

We should always remember our fallen
heroes who paid the price for our
freedom. For their courage and
bravery, we should be ever so humble!

A FINAL TRIBUTE TO THE KNOWN SOLDIER, MICHAEL BLASSIE

You were laid to rest decades in a
monumental tomb. Millions visited
not knowing your name: paying
their respects to one of the great
heroes of our generation.

You didn't know when you were born
that somewhere, in the pages of history
in a distant future, the hand of time
would legibly inscribe your name,
the unknown!

Presidential administrations changed,
wars and rumors of wars occurred in
other countries, and climatic events
happened in America: earthquakes;
hurricanes; tornados; droughts; history
books written; children born; and
children dying in drive-by-shootings not
far from where you were sleeping with
sounds of gunfire disturbing your much
deserved rest.

In July 1998, you were respectfully
removed from Washington and sent
to be identified so your family, friends,
America, and the world could at last
know who you are.

Now, your name is written and sealed
in the heavenly scrolls. You no longer
have to worry about going down in
future history books as an unknown!

At last, you were taken home to your
final resting place to be near
loved ones and friends after being
apart so long. Don't worry, your
family can rest easier. The anguish
may never diminish, but God, in His
infinite mercy, will grant them His
peace.

FIDDLING WITH TIME

Time, I promised I wouldn't fiddle with
you because you're much too serious!
You've given me twenty four hours
for completing tasks. Somehow, I've
procrastinated saying: "tomorrow's
another day!" You haven't promised
me tomorrow. Why do I take you
for granted?

Every second is precious. You keep
ticking away, allowing me another
opportunity for recognizing your rightful
place in my life. When I'm late I blame
you because you didn't wait for me!

Time, will I ever learn you wait for
no one? Days, years, decades, and
centuries have been at your beck-and-
call, and there's no return!

MOUNTAINS OF COURAGE

Some people are courageous during adversities by proving to themselves and others they're in control. These envied, role models appear majestic, secure, and untouchable. They write volumes about their lives without trembling. We should be so lucky!

Are these mountains of courage born or are they unique? When some are running to the hills escaping life's pressures, these individuals are remaining behind securing the fort and keeping out the intruders!

These heroic souls keep families emotionally and spiritually bonded during a crisis. Indeed, we shouldn't lose sight of their frailties, too. However, when their door closes and they're left alone with their memories, how many buckets are overflowing with tears?

THE WINGS OF FAITH

We lose faith when we stop believing in ourselves or others. How sad having no hope! What keeps us going? How do we spiritually sustain ourselves during troubled times?

We're grabbing the wings of faith. When we're clipping them, they're growing back even stronger. If we're holding on tightly and faithfully, they will emotionally balance and spiritually secure us during our darkest moments.

When we're feeling overwhelmed by loneliness, fear, frustration, or apathy, the wings of faith can redirect us back to that flighted path leading to peace!

A MOTHER'S PRAYER TO HER CREATOR

Creator, you've blessed me with
wonderful children who acknowledge
and love you. They were raised with
Christian and moral values which they
learned, respected, and never forgot!

I'd read Bible verses when they were
in their cribs -- even though they didn't
understand. They'd smile as if they
were delighted in hearing Holy Scripture.

When becoming teenagers, they carried
those values and Your Word in their
hearts, safely and securely. I'm grateful
they loved you more than the world.
I pray they'll be forever in Your tender
and loving care.

When life's stormy blows are hitting
them from all directions, and they're in
the midst of danger, let their ascending
prayers protect them.

When they've completed their earthly
tasks, and if it's Your will, let angels
extend a welcoming hand by guiding
them into Your waiting presence!

A HYMN OF PRAISE TO MOTHER NATURE:
A Celebration of God's Handiwork

The Tree

Your grandiose trunk stands firmly rooted in mother nature's soil. You spring forth majestically and towering: spreading your branches, like wings, toward heaven in thanksgiving. For this adoration, we celebrate God's handiwork!

You're constantly amazing us with your strength: ignoring passersby who occasionally gaze upon you breathlessly with awe in their materialistic, hurried pace. God's rain and sunlight is your nourishment. You don't collapse under pressure as people do from their toils and labors. You're a welcoming resting place for birds in their unending flights. Let's praise God for His magnificent creation!

The Grass

You seem to be the most abused of
mother nature's children: people walking
on you in their race going nowhere.
It doesn't matter if you're real or artificial.
Yes, you were here well before we came, and
you'll be here after we're long gone.
So, who's the victor in the end? You
thirst for water because water brings
strength and vitality. We thank Him for His
patience.

The Branch

Your job's important although you're the
bearer of burdens. Everything rests on
your weary branches. For centuries
you've witnessed battles among nations
and other climatic events. Through it
all, you've remained steadfastly. In
nature's grand scheme, we celebrate
our Master's plan.

The Leaf

People admire your beauty, especially
in the fall as you brilliantly display your
rich colors. You hang loosely, ready
for descending at the blow of the wind:
resting on the ground and receiving
God's nourishment from the sun.
For your contribution to mother
nature's creation, we celebrate God's
victory!

LOVING TRIBUTES FROM A SON, HUSBAND, AND FATHER

Part 1. To My Mother

Mom, I know I've told you countless times how much I love you. Somehow, I feel that's not enough! So, your son is writing in celebration of your strength; wisdom; patience; kindness; spirituality; generosity; loyalty; and friendship. Did I leave out anything?

You nourished me from birth, providing moral and spiritual sustenance not found in any milk formula. Evidently, your mother gave you a survival kit for life. Her memories must have had a profound affect on you!

You were comforting when I had my first bruise: nursing and kissing it so gently. While I was crying hysterically, you calmed me with your soft, quiet voice.

When I graduated from high school with honors, your beaming face was seen among hundreds of nervous, anxious parents. I could point you out in the crowd as you brightened the room like the sun. Do you remember when I graduated from college with highest honors? You were there with tears streaming down your face like an unending flood!

When I married, you were the first
offering help, inviting her family to a
cookout. They fell in love with you.
You've always come through for
me, mom.

I've my own family, your grandchildren!
They adore you. They can hardly wait
to visit. They become so excited at the
sound of your name. You're spiritually
and morally feeding them as you did me.
Your grandchildren are the recipients of
your strength. May God bless you with
a long life!

Part 2. To My Wife

Honey, you're the "apple of my eye!"
I admire your qualities of patience;
kindness; gentleness; excitement;
spontaneity; and other outstanding
attributes. I'm constantly expressing
my love daily, bringing gifts for no
apparent reason -- just because I
love you. You've given me hope when
there was none, taught me patience
when I became impatient, and have given
me strength when mine was depleted.
What more can I ask for? Yes, we've
had our ups-and-downs, but through it
all, we weathered the storms in rough
seas.

Part 3. To My Daughter

Daughter, you've brought me happiness
from the day you were born. You looked
so precious then, and you're even more
so, now! I'm proud of your accomplishments.
When your mother's working, you're
pitching right in doing whatever is
necessary when you can be with your
friends at the mall.

Do you remember telling me when you get married,
you're teaching your children the same values you
were taught? You love being home, and your
winning smile lights up any room. You don't like
arguments, and you always want to make things right.

Part 4. To My Son

My son, you look just like me! When you were born
your mother and I argued this point from the
hospital. It doesn't matter who you look like. What's
important is knowing where you came from and where
you're going. You're bright, musical, sensitive, and
caring. I actually think God made you especially for
this family. I'm proud of you. You're a honor
student, a volunteer at the senior citizens' center, and
a tutor for academically challenged students. In fact,
most young men your age would be driving cars and
looking for girls. You love doing things for your
mother and I. You were especially molded for this
family.

In closing, I'd like to thank God for a caring and
appreciative family. May He bless you with His
loving kindness.

A TRIBUTE TO TEACHERS

Teaching is one of the hardest professions. In this climate of academic correctness, it's also one of the hottest professions! Indeed, the profession is honorable, but is often misunderstood by some critics who think teachers are high priced, professional baby-sitters. How quickly they forgot their first teacher!

Parents or guardians are the first teacher. After all, their roles are nurturing, molding, and helping their children develop useful skills and tools necessary for critical thinking.

Teachers are trained, professional educational providers: enhancing and promoting conducive learning environments. The educational pessimists criticizing teachers are the ones who wouldn't dare enter some schools without their legion of armed guards and an armored tank at their disposal for immediate retreat!

Today's teachers are struggling under adverse conditions: deteriorating neighborhoods; gunfire; gang violence; lack of parental support; administration apathy; student apathy; and crumbling structures. In some instances, schools haven't been repaired in decades. (Building code violations, anyone?) Students and teachers are at great risk! How can anyone teach or learn in this environment: worrying when the ceilings are going to collapse, or worse yet, the building?

Would Congress work under these conditions? I don't think so! Well, why should teachers? Proudly, teachers work knowing they've a generation to educate. They aren't in the profession for monetary gain, but for the educational rewards which aren't always immediate. There's even a greater tribute: when students decide to become teachers. What an elation! Now, this is your finest hour. So, find that tee shirt you tucked away that reads: PROUD TO BE A TEACHER!

ARE WE TOO POLITICALLY CORRECT?

Some people think our society is becoming too politically correct. The acceptable community standards a century ago are now undergoing political, correctness surgery! Even the *Holy Bible* is under fire from the radicals and not being spared from the scalpel. For some, terminology reflecting the new millennium should be eradicated: avoiding any sexism or scriptural misinterpretation.

Then again, political correctness should be a personal matter. It isn't a crime having differing views. I'm certain every person wasn't pleased with the political correctness culture of his/her day: the foundations and new ideas challenged by the radicals, the free thinkers. Well, if we stop thinking and debating, we'll cease learning, growing, and nurturing.

We forget there's a generation behind us who'll determine their political correctness destiny. Of course, they're entitled to challenge us like we challenged our previous generation.

Again, are we still too politically correct? Perhaps, biblical scholars, historians, and radical thinkers in the next millennium will leave their recorded indelible impressions for future generations to challenge!

JUST BECAUSE OF MY SEX!

Just because of my sex, I was born at the wrong time. Some men ignored me saying: "I wouldn't amount to anything, but getting married and having a house full of babies!"

Just because of my sex, I was denied playing high school sports reserved for men. It took laws remedying the injustice, but some men blamed me for making waves. They lamented, "why couldn't things remain the same as before?"

Just because of my sex, I was denied entry into one of the most prestigious universities. "We've met our quotas," the admissions committee growled! So, I took extreme measures, and I sued them. Then, some men claimed I was too pushy saying: "why couldn't I wait twenty years -- things will change."

Just because of my sex, the men thought I graduated with highest honors, bribing the professors. "Money talks, they lamented!"

Just because of my sex, the men retorted: "I received special preference to medical school because they didn't have enough women applying."

Just because of my sex, I had first preference for hospital rotation: "ladies first," they shouted throughout the corridors!

Just because of my sex, I could call in sick if I didn't want to do rounds. "She gets away with everything. If we tried that tactic, we'd be canned," the men snapped back!

Just because of my sex, I decided to change my mind and not practice medicine right away. "Her biological time clock must be winding down. All she wants is children." "She wasted a good seat for a male." "I knew this was going to happen," exclaimed my father!

SWEET INNOCENCE

Sweet Innocence whose fragrant
flower reaches toward heaven,
I adore you. Comfort, protect, and
guide me. Your mother's bosom
held you so closely: afraid of
releasing you into the wings of
the dove.

I miss your angelic-like spirit --
now surrounded by choirs of
angels. My heart's in great sorrow!
Why were you taken so young,
gently into the night? Cloak me
with your heavenly protection.

Sweet Innocence: usher in a new
morning filled with brightness,
hope, and peace.

A MARTYR OF THE FAITH

So young, so innocent. Your life wasn't
planned this way. You were supposed
to grow up, become a giant, the pillar in
the community by making us proud!

Somehow, all that changed when you
were sprayed by bullets in a random
drive-by-shooting. Precious one, those
bullets weren't intended for you.
Mommy turned her head for a moment
and then...!

You were gone, instantly, without warning.
There were no farewells. Yes, my precious
fruit, those men were cowards: never
stopping to help, driving erratically, avoiding
being pursued by the police.

Now, I'm beginning my long, laborious
journey into the pit of despair. Will you
ever forgive me? Who will mourn your
passing? Will there be accolades at
your funeral? Truly, you're a martyr of
the faith!

ANGEL OF MERCY

Angel of mercy, you know my burden.
My child was killed so innocently in a
random drive-by-shooting. You
remember him? Yes, he was a martyr
of the faith. I'm leaving him in your
capable hands safely hidden from
harm's way.

He no longer has to worry about the
cares of this world. He's safely snuggled
in your protective wings where no bullets
and no bad men are seeking his life! Don't
forget to tell him -- I love him.

Angel of mercy, give me the strength to
endure. My sheets are soaked from my
tears, my heart is weak from crying, and
my soul is black as midnight. Sit by my
bed while I sleep and gently close my
eyes so I may rest.

Don't leave my side for my grief is
inconsolable. Give me love in my heart
that I may not seek revenge. Lift my feet
so they may walk softly and humbly in
your presence. Steady my trembling
hands so I can reach up in prayer.
Guide my footsteps in the path of
righteousness. Let my lips speak of
your goodness and mercy. At last,
focus my eyes on the Holy Word for
comfort and solace. Amen.

THE HANGMENS' NOOSE!

Internal Revenue, stop squeezing the
   life out of me.
The burdens and stresses of working
   are killing me!

My household is in turmoil. My son's
   in jail.
My daughter's six months pregnant,
   and my life's a living hell!

My accountant is frantic and the codes
   aren't clear.
She's off learning the new laws,
   trembling in fear!

I'm called to the office, it seems
   so unclear.
When the auditors shout out to me:
   "an audit is near!"

Single people in our family don't have
   a wing and a prayer.
They're all hoping the IRS will help
   their despair!

The smokers in my family are
   puffing today. As for taxing
   their habit, it won't blow away!

Lord, give me the strength at
   least to complain.
To the IRS who bear no blame!

THESE HALLOWED HALLS ON CAPITOL HILL

These hallowed halls are sacred and
revered by those who pass through
them with the respectability and sanctity
of a great cathedral whose beauty
swallows us with its echoing vastness.

Confidential secrets have been kept.
Many have eavesdropped on the small
and the great of these trampled halls:
its occupants vowing their fidelity.

Many triumphant occasions have been
witnessed: dignitaries, including kings
and queens; princes and princesses; the
wise and the unwise; the respected
religious; the rich and the poor; the
entertainers; the just and the unjust;
the happy and the sad; the gays and
the straights; the loved and the unloved;
the saints and the sinners, and most of
all, the pets whose paws have graced
these hallowed halls. Many politicians
have walked slowly; hurriedly, patiently;
impatiently; eagerly; indecisively;
nervously; or somberly. These halls
have heard debates, compromises,
and final decisions affecting its
constituents.

Reportings of assassinations and
impeachments, numbing the American
public and the world, have echoed
throughout these majestic corridors.

These hallowed halls have heard
children playing and running through its
corridors, exploring their new home
away from home.

Finally, these halls have been cleaned,
refreshed, and renewed with the spirit
of patriotism. Let these hallowed halls
forever be a symbol of America's
greatness!

WHAT DID YOU SAY YOUR NAME WAS, AGAIN?

Why are you wearing a name tag? Have you forgotten your name? Oh, I know, you have amnesia! While some people have excellent memories, mine isn't too bad -- if the name is easy. If it's more than seven letters (seven is supposed to be my lucky number), then memorizing names becomes challenging! Word association is always helpful, too. If I don't remember a name, I literally go through the alphabet.

I know you've been to conventions and noticed those sterile-like badges greeting you with their favorite greeting, hello! Everyone wants his or her name remembered without me or anyone else asking: "what did you say your name was, again?"

On the other hand, it could be the aging process. What's wrong with me? At this stage in my life, I'm lucky if I know my name! Hey, most people wouldn't change their name. Unfortunately, it's not free. Imagine the courts charging for a name change. What's this country coming to?

Remembering the days of yore (and I'm not going to mention how many), I was sharp-witted with an almost computer-like memory, and I didn't have to write anything down. By the way, I had my mental calendar, could plan almost six-months in advance, and remember every event. (I confess: that was before twenty-five. After that, it's been a downhill struggle.) Well, we're coming into a new millennium, and I'll be meeting interesting people and learning new names. Pardon me, what did you say your name was, again?

A TOUCH OF CLASS

Don't you just want to take these people home and mold them into your own image? These individuals possess a touch of class! They're everywhere: churches; malls; supermarkets; streets; families; television; parks; work; department stores; urban cities; small towns; apartments; and condominiums.

They aren't necessarily rich as you don't have to be rich to be classy. The classiest people are those who aren't rich, who don't wear the finest clothes, or drive the fanciest cars. When entering a room, there's "something" about them that exudes class: whether it's confidence, posture, or charm.

Most people think of movie stars as being classy, and in fact, some are. Well, having class comes from within. Is it a certain look? Do classy people strut differently from the rest? These are some challenging questions to consider. Hum, I'm always stopping in my tracks when I see classy people! (A smidgen of class can go a long way).

So when you see people with a touch of class: stop, look, and appreciate them because they're a rarity and should be admired. Excuse me, could I borrow a touch of class?

IN RECOGNITION OF OUR SENIOR CITIZENS:
Accolades Long Overdue

Senior citizens, I apologize for not recognizing you earlier. Your accolades are long overdue, too. You're valuable to us. Your wisdom, experience, and perseverance can't be bought and discarded like a loaf of bread!

You're committing yourselves to family, neighbors, community, and friends. You don't ask anything in return but to be needed and valued. In an age of youth and their dreams, we sometimes forget about your aspirations. Three score twenty and ten doesn't mean life is over. You've just begun to live!

There's more to your life than B-I-N-G-O and WHEEL OF FORTUNE, both games of chance! You haven't survived just on luck alone, but by observations and learning from your mistakes. Your experiences are rich. You can actually write your autobiography and some are doing that. Your enthusiasm for life is contagious. You're giving counsel, hope, and happiness to a materialistic generation. Age isn't a factor. In fact, you use age to your advantage. You're competing in marathons; enrolling in adult education classes; taking college courses for credit; mentoring; writing books; novels; poems; taking flying lessons; skiing; enrolling in culinary arts; square dancing; calligraphy classes; volunteering at various agencies; and a willing participant in other endeavors.

Believe me, this isn't an exhaustive list of your accomplishing feats, but you aren't afraid to be all that you can be! You aren't complaining about time because you savor life's sweet banquet, a fitting feast for you.

When the epilogue is legibly inscribed in your book of life, let the moving hand of time write: you weren't afraid to live life richly!

A TRIBUTE TO THE STATUE OF LIBERTY

Miss Liberty, you're standing gracefully
welcoming the weary and heavy laden.
You're offering a hearty greeting to
everyone regardless of political
affiliation; religion; race; creed; color;
sexual preference; or natural origin.

You're seeing countless ships entering
and leaving, but you aren't complaining
because you're always maintaining your
poise and composure even in inclement
weather.

How many tears are you shedding seeing
excited immigrants? Do you weep when
they weep?

Occasionally, you need restoration due
to pollution and other circumstances
beyond your control. Through it all,
you don't complain because you love
seeing happy smiles on childrens' faces.

When night approaches, this is the
time you radiate: glowing and
bestowing your hospitality to all
seeking refuge.

You belong to the people, and you
can't budge from your permanent
fixture because you love them.

Keep standing tall and erect and may
God bless you, Miss Liberty!

THIS ENCHANTING CITY: Albuquerque, New Mexico

Albuquerque, you extended a warm
welcome when I first visited. I fell
in love with your people, mountains,
and spaciousness: a richness
undefined and undefiled by its
inhabitants.

Your diverse culture is contagious,
giving your city a charm of its own,
cueing on the diverse ethnic groups
who comprise this wonderful and
exuberant cosmopolitan mixture:
providing a uniqueness and a stable
quality to this enchanting city.

Visitors are summoned from coast-to-
coast by these enchanting mountains
and mesmerizing sunsets: a visitors' rite
of passage where blaring trumpets can be
heard beckoning them to enter with
great fanfare and style!

Albuquerque, I adore you. May I ever
bring favor and faithfulness to you for
being so wonderfully kind to a stranger
passing through.

At last, I've heard the great trumpets,
and they've beckoned me to stay and
contribute to this enchanting city!

IN THE BLEAK MIDWINTER: NEW YORK CITY REVISITED

I used to live on the east coast, and I can attest it's bitterly cold, especially in New York City. Sure, the tall buildings shield you from the wind, but once you turn those unforgiving corners, the winds can be unmerciful. Of course, New York has a crispness in the air, too. Most people actually come alive: not that they were dead before!

Christmas is a great time to visit, or anytime, especially when you're seeing smiling faces or frowning ones (if they're broke from spending).
 Listening to the greatest organs from the finest churches, most notably, Saint Thomas Church Fifth Avenue, a large gothic Episcopal Church located at West 53rd Street & Fifth Avenue, is a music lover's dream.

The choir of men and boys is still a rare treat in North America, and there's only one word to describe them: breathtaking! This visit must be a part of your itinerary. Believe me, you won't regret it. I used to be a parishioner, pew 256 (my personal choice), and I never regretted it for one moment. You see, I was a creature of habit. Now, for the residents or want-to-be residents: having a fireplace is a blessing (almost next to sainthood). People kill, not literally, for that additional perk! There's something magical and complementary about a fireplace: warmth and friendship. Somehow, some people are more romantic with the right setting, background music, a special attraction to a brisk evening.

I haven't witnessed many blizzards, but I do recall two: one in the 70s and one in the 90s. New York never sleeps, and it usually doesn't close for business. Those two blizzards were the only exceptions. However, the city opened its operations within a week. Everyone came together and "took care of business!" I must give New York credit: in a crisis the people stick together. That was especially true during the blackout during the 80s. Amazingly, strangers came to the aid of other strangers as if they were friends. This is quite remarkable in a city that large with the reputation for being cold, aloof, and unkind, depending upon your sources.

For me, I felt it was time for a change having lived in North Carolina and New Jersey. Then I ventured to New Mexico. Believe me, it's really, really different -- almost a 360° turn. New York is fast paced: lively, energetic, and happening. However, if you're living in the biggest city in New Mexico, its energy is somewhat different: laid back, friendly, scenic, and spiritual. It's hard to describe unless you've visited here or have lived here. Nevertheless, the crowds in New York are entertaining with an astonishing "get-me-to-the-theatre-on-time" attitude. Presently, I'm enjoying the southwest. I don't know where my crystal ball will take me, but I'm prepared to venture. By the way, we don't have the cold, severe winters, but I can always dream about New York, New York that wonderful town!

SWEET, SOFT SUMMER RAIN

I love the smell of rain as it drips on nature and humanity with refreshing moisture. The rain sometimes surprises us with torrential downpours, causing delayed plans, and reminding us who's in charge. In our hurried lives, we often take nature for granted by not pausing and reflecting its magnificent wonder.

There's a time and a place for everything under the sun, even the rain. Nature balances beautifully whether or not we understand its intention. Who are we to question its purpose?

THE FLOWERS OF MY YOUTH!

Sweet, short days gone by like
flowers whose birth came
unannounced. The smell of roses;
sunflowers; petunias; daisies; daffodils;
morning glories; and lilies shooting
toward heaven: searching for sunlight
and soaking in God's rays!

I, too, once sprung up like a flower
waiting to be held, nurtured, and loved.
My, how the time quickly escaped my
memory: a memory of past days gone
by when gentle breezes and soft
nights caressed and held me in their
arms until morning! Yet, time hadn't
been too kind. It flew by so quickly,
abandoning me and leaving me desolate!

Now, the twilight of my youth has
wrestled its way into my life unexpectedly.
Yet, I must cherish each moment by
living life richly: before twilight closes the
drawn curtains, never to be opened again!

THE GIFT OF LIFE!

Your birth wasn't an accident because you were conceived in love, not resentment! When we first saw you, your innocent eyes sparkled and illuminated the sterile ward: while the morning sun caught a glimpse of your timely arrival!

Then, your screams echoed throughout the rounded corridors and bounced off the complacent mountains as they awaited your arrival, breathlessly!

Toys, balloons, stuffed animals, and good cheer welcomed you in this your grand and festive entrance into mother nature's embrace!

Soon, your baby-babble will turn to anticipation of melodious sounds of joy and happiness as you phrase your way into your new world!

Your gift of life will bring us hope for a brighter day and a promise of a better tomorrow!

WHEN GOD MADE WOMAN

When God made woman, He molded
her for greatness with her tenderness,
compassion, and loving nature: calling
earth's grand reception to receive her
enlightened spirit.

Her dust was sprinkled from heaven
bringing happiness and peace on the
troubled earth. Her spirituality was
endowed by her Creator as a gift to
the world for the healing of the nations.

Yet, her burdens had been heavy as
she bore the weight of the world on her
misunderstood shoulders: childbearing,
pain, and suffering for the fulfillment of
The Gospel.

This proud woman whose children
suckled from nature's best...rested
wearily from days' toils and sorrows.
Who dared questioned her laments
begging for a lighter cross? There
was no Simon of Cyrene standing
by the wayside carrying her cross!

She patiently and lovingly continued
her long, laborious struggles with
searching eyes for any sign of respite
from her Heavenly Father who knows
how much she can bear, but won't
leave her comfortless.

THOUGHTS OF YOU

My thoughts of you ache to be
touched by your warm, seductive
hands because I'm separated from
your presence.

Everyday is like a thousand years
without you: as time seems to stand
still in silence for the night to hide my
pillow soaked tears!

My love, when your thoughts sparkle
in my mind, my heart's scorched by
your passionate flame which will never
be extinguished by time or eternity.

My thoughts of you won't drown as a
sinking vessel. Instead, our love will
be carried out to sea while the winds
blow to unknown destinations no one
can reach, and where we'll vanish into
the darkness of time!

THE LAST TIME I SAW YOU!

The last time I saw you -- you were
beautiful like an evening breeze.
Your freshness permeated the room
like the smell of cut roses without
the thorns!

The last time I saw you, tears fell from
your face like morning dew waiting for
the sun to warm its sleepy state!

The last time I saw you -- you loved
earnestly by disregarding your feelings
and loving me without any reservations!

The last time I saw you, your eyes
glistened like sparkling champagne
to be gracefully sipped and savored
for the right occasion!

The last time I saw you, there was
joy exuded by your presence because
you were so full of life. You wanted
to share that exuberance with me!

The last time I saw you, you were
willing to renew our wedding vows
because you wanted to reaffirm our
commitment -- for better or for worse.

IF I HAD TO DO IT OVER AGAIN, I'D

Smell the flowers and breathe in God's
    fragrance.

Have a pleasant smile and not a frown
    for a stranger I don't know.

Look toward heaven and thank God
    for His creation.

Watch innocent children play with one
    another without fear or prejudice.

Appreciate my blessings without
    envying my neighbors'
    possessions.

Smell the cold mist off the ocean
    waves as the waves slam against
    the rocks.

Help when I see an abused child.

Take sleep more seriously as some
    have trouble sleeping.

Not take sight for granted. There are
    those who can't see.

Hear and appreciate the melodious
    sounds of robins. There are many
    unable to hear.

Touch your sweet thoughts if I could
    because you're always on my mind.

Drink from nature's spring without
    complaining. There are those
    whose lips are sealed in death.

Embrace a family member: it could
    be the last time.

Hug my friends and thank them for
    their emotional support because
    some people are friendless.

Ask God for His richest blessings
    because some never got the
    chance.

Appreciate and respect my neighbors'
    sexual orientation without being
    judgmental.

Read and appreciate the known and
    unknown authors for their diligence
    and patience in producing the
    written word.

Exercise and eat healthier because some
    have heart by-pass operations due to
    clogged arteries.

Climb every mountain until I find
    my dream.

Take the time to love
    without the fear of being hurt.

Say Amen more after the sermon by
   giving the minister spiritual support.
   S/he has one of the most
   challenging vocations: serving God
   and doing His will.

DETOUR FROM MY HEART

Love struck me like a sharp, pointed
arrow while I wasn't looking. I was slightly
distracted. When deflecting the blow,
the arrow detoured from my heart,
landing on the pavement of disillusionment.

When I see you, my heart throbs violently
as if it were exploding from your very
touch. Walking toward me, I'm as giddy
as a school girl waiting for her books to
be carried by that special someone.

How I long to have those straight, love
arrows aiming at my heart again without
detouring: leaving behind traces of your
existence. When picking up the broken
tips, remember I stood in your path only
to be marked and targeted.

I'll miss you knowing you've places to go.
There are other arrows to be tested and
retested until you hit that perfect heart!

REMEMBER?

Remember meeting on our first date?
You were so lovely and radiant
standing on your parents' porch next
to the freshly, painted white swing.

Remember the lecture hall for
English 101? You were in row three,
seat eight, nervously awaiting the
professor's lecture.

Remember meeting in the campus
library? I was watching you from the
corner of my eye while trying to
concentrate.

Remember anxiously waiting for the
posting of the final grades? I was
standing next to you, speechless!

Remember graduating from college?
You with highest honors: me with high
honors. You kept complimenting
my grand achievement while forgetting
your own.

Remember being accepted at The
University of New Mexico Law
School, Albuquerque? You had
always wanted to be a lawyer since
you were a little girl.

Remember graduating from law
school and receiving honors? I was
ecstatic and you were crying
uncontrollably.

Remember proposing to you? You
were so surprised, shouting: "yes!"

Remember our first child, a boy? You
were excited at the prospect of
motherhood.

Remember our twins, two girls:
making our family complete?

Remember when our children said
their first words? You began recording
this momentous event for future
generations.

Remember when the childrens'
grandparents took them for ice cream?
The children were thrilled being
with them.

Remember the children growing up
so fast and becoming parents
themselves? Where did the time go?

Remember doting on our grandchildren,
spoiling them with every conceivable
toy they could possibly imagine?

Remember retiring and planning on
travelling extensively? Well, that dream
came true.

Remember when our hopes and dreams
became realities because we loved and
respected each other? Honey, thank
you for being there for me. I love you
dearly!

TIDAL BOUT

Resting against a dilapidated pier on
a breezy, spring day surrounded by
gorgeous, sculptured-like seagulls, my
eyes are fixed on the splashing,
churning blue waves seemingly
competing for first place.

Their competitive nature appears
real...as in a boxing ring. Who'll be
the victor in this bout to reach shore?
I can hear the thrashing sounds of clashing
waves, bashing one another. They seem to
be almost dancing!

Over, under, around they go: jostling
for tidal position. For them -- it's
power. Faintly, they're saying: "may
the better wave win!"

In this corner...! "Now, it's my turn to
beat the crap out of you," the opponent
yells! Tossing and flipping their
vivacious, curved-liked waves, they
reach land announcing their climatic
arrival. "Gee, it's good to be home,
isn't it? "I'm exhausted after that
fight," sighs the victor. Pounding their
last breath, they rest wearily embracing
and giving tidal support, an act of
mutual friendship and comfort. "Don't
get too closely." "On our way back, I'm
still kicking some tidal butt," the
victor exclaims!

TRUE TO OURSELVES!

We were taught as children that lying was wrong, and telling the truth was always better for our soul and backside! That's great advice. Did we forget that great lesson as we became adolescents and adults?

Do we think too highly of ourselves by thinking we're God's greatest gift? We sometimes lie to ourselves and others by shielding and protecting our inadequacies.

There's no law against not being true to ourselves. To the unknowing public, we're cool, calm, and in control. We're actually impostors! If our mirror could talk, it would speak volumes of truths about us. We'd gladly shatter it without picking up the broken pieces because most of us enjoy the deception, acting out our fantasies. We don't need to rent a clown, we're the clown.

I know it's hard work being painfully honest because it's an unpleasant and thankless job. There are no incentives and rewards for doing great. However, if we're really truthful our distorted mirror will reassemble itself like a scattered puzzle. Pieces of our deceptive lives will painstakingly and patiently be put back together because we would've done some serious introspection without fear of rejection.

FRANKLY SPEAKING!

Frankly speaking, you must be painfully
honest. You can't fool anyone but
yourself! Are you afraid of the truth,
the consequences, or not knowing
at all? You're the biggest loser if you're
hiding from yourself.

Why are you running, avoiding life's
hurdles and stumbling blocks? Aren't
you aware of the stop sign ahead?
Life's red light isn't going to change.
Your feet are permanently cemented
to the ground until you can face your
tomorrows, frankly speaking!

Are you calling for help? There's no one
hearing your cries. They're running the
race toward victory having faced life's
major obstacles, pushing them aside,
running to the finish line, and winning
the prize.

The prize can't be purchased in any
store, put away on a layaway plan, or
charged to your credit card. No one
can go in your place. You must be
present to receive it. The prize is
called h-o-n-e-s-t-y!

THOSE LONG SUMMER NIGHTS

Those long summer nights and gentle
breezes are a reminder of lost days
gone by when we were young and
fanciful.

The earth's trodden soil where our
footsteps once trod lies sunken in
time, never to be unearthed.

I begged those long summer nights
not to end: the beginning of our time
had just begun to illuminate the skies
when night descended upon us.

Then, those long summer nights
skipped for joy as they played along
the shores of time: not regarding
time as its enemy -- but as a friend.

Now, our time has ended and those
long summer nights must go into
hiding once more: sleeping until
summoned again from earth's pall.

WHAT'S HAPPINESS?

Happiness is being loved by someone
    you love.

Happiness is a forbidden rose in bloom.

Happiness is friendship and loyalty
    without the demands.

Happiness is the gleam in your
    lover's eyes.

Happiness is feeling good about
    yourself and outwardly exuding
    that warmth.

Happiness is holding an innocent baby
    in your protective arms.

Happiness is the aroma of your
    lover's natural perfume.

Happiness is lying in the dark:
    in wordless dialogue.

Happiness is peace of mind.

Happiness is touching your warm
    body on a cold winter's night.

Happiness is sometimes not explainable
    in words but by actions.

PRICELESS TREASURE

You, my priceless treasure, have been
with me through many adversities,
weathering life's challenging storms
without warning. Our relationship has
been like a trickle of water, a torrential
downpour, and an unexpected flood!

Somehow, we've survived without
rescue from family, friends, or
neighbors. Our prayers and faith
sustained us when other avenues
failed.

You're more priceless than an
emerald. You can't be replaced
like a damaged picture whose
edges have been worn by time.
Time isn't a natural enemy --
but tomorrow's greeting with you
by my side.

I'll always cherish you, my priceless
treasure. When I was in the depths of
depression, you disregarded your
frailties. Now, I'm publicly bestowing
this deserving tribute.

REFLECTING ON THE JOYS OF CHILDHOOD

My, how the years have flown and much too quickly. Sweet memories of grandma's fresh hot bread with that come-and-eat-me dough, rising and spilling over like a bubbling volcano waiting to explode without warning!

Life seemed much simpler. Inflation wasn't the dinner conversation, but wholesome family discussions were encouraged. Back then the family ate, prayed, and stayed together. There weren't drive-by-shootings, people weren't ducking for cover, and there weren't dress rehearsals for life.

There were toys in the driveways, children playing without fear, and neighbors watching out for one another. We used to call them nosy. Today, life's much too complex: no more innocently skipping through the park; playing hide-and-seek; playing mommy and daddy (some are without the marriage license); or casually bicycling through unknown, or for that fact, known neighborhoods. Sadly, this generation has lost that innocence we once loved and cherished.

WHEN TIMES WERE GOOD

When times were good, we loved, lived, and learned from each other. Everyday was spring for us: filled with hope, renewal, and a promise of a better tomorrow.

We lived life by enjoying little pleasures, and it didn't cost us but our time: walking briskly in the park; catching a glimpse of a fading sunset; riding our bikes like little children in a competition; and enjoying the wonders of nature, a squirrel hiding its nuts in anticipation of a much deserved feast.

Our love was undeniably ours to be cherished and sustained by us alone without any outside intervention. We respected each other's likes and dislikes. There was always room for compromise. Sometimes a tender look in your eyes was all I needed to confirm you loved me!

When times were good, life was our game of chance and the world our playpen. We enjoyed flirting with our game board to determine where our moves would eventually land: stop or go!

When times were good, we had to keep going as we couldn't stop because the hand of time would record its last message.

Denise Michelle Phillips

We stood by the shores of time waiting
for the waves to take us so we could
be swept away by the currents, never to
be seen again!

AN ACT OF KINDNESS!

Your warm smile brightened my day
as my thoughts weren't of you, but on
myself, an introvert by nature.
An act of kindness, I'll never forget!

You saw through my mask, and taking
a chance, you spoke first hoping I'd
graciously respond. I smiled accepting
your genuine greeting. An act of
kindness, I'll never forget!

A greeting from you in the hallway,
elevator, or laundry room restored my
faith in humankind in a world where
there's so much skepticism and
pessimism. An act of kindness, I'll
never forget!

In a church filled with strangers and
awaiting the morning's sermon, your
friendly welcome gave me pause:
reflecting on the Creator's blessings,
and His servants who joyfully spread
the Good News of His love. An act of
kindness, I'll never forget!

In this hurried pace of "me-firsts," and
"later-for-you" attitudes, you circumvent
those acceptable societal norms by
extending your hand, helping me cross
troubled waters, and keeping me from
drowning. An act of kindness, I'll
never forget!

I'M JUST A STRANGER PASSING THROUGH!

I'm nameless because I do things for
others without praise or fanfare.
You'll never hear joyous church bells
tolling for me or state trumpets
echoing from the great cathedrals.
I'm just a stranger passing through!

I'll even respectfully decline radio and
television interviews. You won't see
photographers in my driveway for
the picture of the moment because
I'm just a stranger passing through!

My family respects my wishes:
they don't give interviews. They're
much too modest. They don't want to be
bombarded by the media so sought after
by our pseudo culture. They've taught
me how to be a stranger passing through!

I give anonymously to charities and
attend benefits incognito: sitting near
the exit and leaving undetected because
I'm just a stranger passing through!

When the books are closed and the
final chapter is written, let my epitaph
read: "here lies a stranger passing
through!"

NOBODY LOVES ME!

What's wrong with me? Just because
I was facially disfigured at fourteen
doesn't mean I'm not worthy of anyone.
I often feel nobody loves me!

I remember the taunts, laughs, and
stares. Some people asked me
personal, insensitive questions. My
parents lashed out at them for their
ignorance.

I'm convincing myself that time heals
all wounds, but for me, my physical
wounds won't heal. I must wear this
mask forever, a mask of torment and
ridicule by those who don't want to
know me. The operations were
painful and unbearable.

Why can't I find a man to love me?
I've needs, too. I'm warm, caring,
sensitive, intelligent, and humorous.
My humor has helped me cope with
my challenge.

I've many supportive friends who
knew me before my accident and
have remained loyal. If it weren't
for them, I'd be alone. They've
been my anchor during troubled
times. Sure, they love me on a
different level, but I'm searching
for a more personal, intimate
relationship.

Since I don't drive, my friends take me with them. I've dated, but the boys never call back. They seemed ashamed to be seen with me. How I wish someone would take the time to know me by not judging the outside, but by judging my character!

SOMEBODY'S CHILD

Somebody's child is crying because
she was supposed to be nurtured,
loved, and protected. Now, child,
your hopes and dreams are dashed.
The streets are the guardians of your
soul. Will your prayers and wails go
unanswered?

The protectors of your soul
abandoned you: a victim of a
cold, uncaring, and greedy
society whose grasp for worldly
pleasures ignored your pleas for
protection. Who deceived your
unknowing eyes?

Where's your new home? Under a
bridge; cardboard box; in a shelter;
friend's house; park; abandoned car;
anywhere? Don't think we don't
understand your lot. Your cross is
heavy with our shame!

Your departure wasn't planned like an
airplane flight because your home
wasn't a safe haven. You're not
responsible for your dysfunctional
environment. You'd erase all social
ills from your memory if you could!

Our punishment is swift and near.
We'll be judged by God for ignoring
you. You gave us warning signs.
Our eyes were clouded by our
fear, selfishness, and pride. Can you
ever forgive us?

MY ENEMIES ARE SEEKING MY SOUL!

I wasn't taught to be strong. I've fought battles all my life and won because my opponents were waging war against my soul. I trusted them with my battle armor off, and they used my weakness obtaining victory. I wandered through the wilderness fortnightly while my enemies sought after me with lance and shield!

Now, the battle lines are drawn. My enemies are charging toward me in their displeasure. They're seeking my soul. I'm yielding my spirit to God whose breath will resurrect me out of my languidness. Quickly, I'm charging toward my opponents with vigor and renewed strength by slaying them with the sword of righteousness!

My enemies are disintegrating like dry bones and returning to the earth from whence they came. They're lying and waiting for their next ambush, conquering the unexpected, the unguarded whose days are short and few. My God, let not my enemies seek my soul. They're seeking pleasure in the weak like a baby without a mother's protection. Restore this natural sleep so I may rest: embraced by eternity where my enemies will rise no more!

BETRAYED

I opened the entrance doors of my life
as you revolved around me from
day-to-day. Endless days gone by
without a call or even a card. Your
voice so distant echoes in my ears.

I trusted you so lovingly: my heart,
soul, and life. You used me like an
expired credit card, tossing me away
after your last purchase!

Did you once think I would relive those
sleepless nights without you? Had it
occurred to you...love was like fine
wine? The longer it aged, the better
it became.

Too short, too short -- my conscience
reminded me -- baffled by mixed
emotions. No, I didn't want to know
the truth. The pain and the indignation
would've been unbearable.

At last, time erased all traces of your
existence. You soared like an eagle
to unknown challenges. As for me, I'm
alone...but not lonely!

MOMMY, WHERE'S DADDY?

Part 1. Daddy's Working

Mommy, where's daddy? Daddy's working trying to support us by the sweat of his brow! You know, I'm glad you asked. Let me tell you how I met him. I was attending law school, and he was sitting next to me. I think it was seat 125. While the professor lectured, he'd occasionally sneak a glance, smiling and winking at the same time. Looking back on those moments, I was as giddy as a little girl. He was (and still is) a very, handsome man.

After graduating from law school, he found a prestigious position in a law firm. I worked at another well established firm when, after several dates, he proposed marriage. Honey, I couldn't say no to a man like that. I fell in love with him after several dates. I quit work after we married because I wanted children and to be a stay-at-home mom during your formative years. You're a blessed event in our lives. Well, our marriage had its ups-and-downs. However, we pledged our loyalty to each other. This is where we now stand!

Part 2. Your Daddy Wants A Separation

Mommy, where's daddy? Listen my child, your daddy wants a separation. While he's sleeping, I'm lying awake thinking what could've gone wrong. Oh no, I'm not blaming myself. Although we've been married ten years (it doesn't seem that long), we somehow became sidetracked. He wanted me to return to work. I didn't want to because I felt you needed me. We had discussions about this...then arguments! There weren't any physical fights. So, we decided on a separation, since we weren't coming to an amicable solution.

We felt we needed a cooling off period, and we'd start over again -- like newlyweds. He didn't want you to see him leaving. So, he left out the back while you were playing in the front yard. My loving eyes watched you so innocently with tears running down like a broken dam! I tried consoling myself with these comfortable words: he'll return!

Part 3. Your Father Wants A Divorce

Mother, where's father? My dear, you've grown up so beautifully, a teenager now. You've made me proud: a honor student; an outstanding athlete; a junior acolyte in our church; and a volunteer at the senior citizen's center. I'll always love and adore you.

I know you're busy with so many activities. Do you have some time to spend? Sit down, please. I received a letter from your father's attorney. He wants a divorce! Trembling, crying, and attempting to regain my composure, I had to sit and think...how do I plan our lives. Sure, he's willing to pay child support, but your feelings must be taken into consideration, too.

Your father loves you. You've often told me life goes on. You're so wise at fifteen. Sometimes, your maturity frightens me. I'm returning back to work, and after school, you can stay at your aunt's house until I return. We'll survive this crisis!

Part 4. Your Father's Remarrying

Mother, where's father, now? Honey, your father's remarrying, starting a new family. He wrote inviting us to his wedding: how thoughtful! I hold no grudges. I'm wishing him God's speed and the best of luck with his new family. Since you've always wanted to go to college, your father provided a college fund. Don't worry about me, I'll do just fine. I've been promoted to senior partner in my law firm. It looks like I've a bright future! I'm concerned about you, though.

Part 5. Your Father Has Passed Away

Mother, where's father? We haven't heard from him lately. You know, since I've my own family, I've been keeping busy. I used to drop by and see you at least twice a week, but medical school is challenging. Oh, I'm sorry to monopolize the conversation. You were saying...?

Please sit. I've something to tell you. Your father passed away this morning! I was hoping you would drop by, but I didn't want a tragedy to be our coffee discussion. Again, I know you love him. You were daddy's girl. If you feel like talking, or if you want to be alone, I'll understand. [You do want to talk.] Well, his wife wants us to attend his funeral and sit with the family. You know he had three children. We both have fond memories of him, don't we? You've always kept a photo album filled with his pictures. Let's look through them together. Hopefully, the pictures will bring us some consolation.

Do you remember your first birthday? Oh, what am I talking about -- you don't remember. Well, it was grand. You had a big party with balloons, a clown, and lots of presents. Your cousins were there, too. You were grinning with that same beautiful smile you now have. It seems almost like yesterday. I made a special outfit for you: a pink ruffled dress with a pink bow placed on the left side of your beautiful black curly hair. Guess what, I cut a lock off and saved it for you. I thought you might want to show it to your grandchildren.

Let's skip ahead: when you were five, you were speaking phrases and asking questions. You didn't know then, but you were a gifted child. It was amazing the things that came from your mouth. "Mommy, when will I become a doctor?" or "Mommy, are all mothers as pretty as you?" Your father, too, was shocked: smiling and proclaiming loudly: "that's my girl!"

When you were ten, you were growing up like a bean stalk: tall, eloquent in your movements, and model-like features. Even the ten year old boys were admiring you from a distance.

However, you used to say: "silly boys, what do they know!" You always had an answer. Your father and I saw so much promise in you, and you never disappointed us in the least.

At age eleven, you had skipped a couple of grades. The teachers said that you were brilliant. Your report card reflected your academic dreams: you were always an "A" student. However, you felt you hadn't achieved your highest goals. You wanted to be the very best. Of course, we always told you we'd be proud of you if you made "Bs," but that wasn't good enough for you. Your expectations were our expectations, and we never pushed you.

When you were thirteen, you were voted most likely to succeed in middle school. You were so popular and bright -- even back then. Your father and I dreamed of that moment when you'd gracefully glide across the mahogany floor to receive your award. Do you remember the thunderous applause and the standing ovation?

If your father could only sit down with us and go down memory lane. You're blushing now, relishing the moment when your father gave you a beautiful engraved silver necklace and a matching bracelet. You jumped for joy -- almost in his arms from the excitement. What a day to remember!

Now, you're an adult, and we're finally closing the book, but not the memories. I don't know if we'll ever find closure. Sure, we must go through our personal grieving stages. For you, I don't know how long it'll take. For me, I can't even begin to say because we had some fond memories sharing them with you. May his soul rest in peace!

THE FARMERS' MARKET

The farmers' market is a real treat
for the unsuspected and the daring
who venture into its path filled with
flirtatious, colorful vegetables, fruits,
breads, jams, and honeys for loving
and consuming.

The farmers' market is filled with
passersby who glance right and left
for fear of missing out on the wonderful
natural aromas from an array of baskets
bursting with pride.

The farmers' market is a place to meet
and greet strangers whose smiles and
conversations bring that special unpaid,
unrehearsed joy and laughter.

The farmers' market is sometimes
where dogs run freely, playing with
one another for the first time
regardless of sex or breed.

The farmers' market is a natural friend
of the people who anticipate its arrival
every year with the old and the new:
bringing with it a luxury we sometimes
take for granted!

A BUS CALLED ANYWHERE

I watch excited passengers at the
bus station purchasing tickets like a child
who's seeing his/her grandparents for the
first time.

There are endless conversations among
people who have never met, but seem as
if they've known one another for years.

Bus destinations announced: one-by-one
they're boarding eagerly and hurriedly
going somewhere.

I'm boarding later to anywhere where
people are willing to embrace me among
the famous and infamous even for a
flashing moment!

GOD, WHAT AM I DOING HERE?
(Dedicated to the residents at all correctional facilities)

I didn't mean to kill him. The gun just
accidentally went off. This is my first
offense and during the sentencing the
judge showed no mercy: "fifty years,"
he shouts! God, what am I doing here?

The penal system is so unfair. There
are criminals committing crimes this
very hour. Some of them are just
lucky, I guess. As for me, I was
caught, prosecuted, and convicted by
a jury of my peers. Have they any
compassion? God, what am I doing
here?

Don't the lawyers, judges, and jury
know I've a family, too. I've left them
unloved and unprotected without a
father and a husband. God, what am
I doing here?

My young friends told me to
get back on track, but I wouldn't
listen to their advice. Impatiently,
I answered: "you're too young, what
do you know about life?" "You've
barely lived yourself!" God, what am
I doing here?

I'm told when to eat, rec, sleep,
shower, and dress. Can't they let me
think. I've a mind of my own. God,
what am I doing here?

The other residents are taking their
sentences in stride. I can't seem to
forget that fatal night. It's almost
like a dream: being at the wrong place
at the wrong time! God, what am I
doing here?

The parole board won't consider an
early release because of my crime.
Time-and-time again, they're
ignoring my pleas. God, what am I
doing here?

Anxiously, I'm awaiting the morning
mail. Maybe, an officer will soon yell,
"mail call!" I'm hoping a letter will be
mine, letting me know my family loves
me. God, what am I doing here?

I'm looking from behind these bars
watching children play: reminding me
of my childhood and how free I was.
God, what am I doing here?

There are residents coming and going
as they're paroled: laughing, screaming,
and crying for joy. I'm wondering if the
system will remember me. A governor's
pardon will do in this season of good will
toward men! God, what am I doing here?

GOD, I'M NOT ANGRY AT YOU!

Sometimes, I ask why circumstances
are the way they are without thinking:
who am I to question His goodness
and mercy. God, I'm not angry at you!

There has been many sudden deaths:
mother, father, grandmother, and
grandfather. I don't know how much
I can bear. God, I'm not angry at you!

Even young children are innocent
victims of street violence. They aren't
to blame for a dysfunctional person's
mad rage. Where's the justice?
Who cares about them in a world
with so much fear, hatred, and
violence that even love can't
balance the scales of justice,
compassion, and mercy. God, I'm
not angry at you!

I hear EMS sirens wailing outside
my bedroom window, and I'm
praying their next victim is a false
alarm. A mother's prayer is
answered: not this time. God, I'm
not angry at you!

The mortuary vehicle is in front of
my neighbor's building: crowds
rubbernecking for a glance at a
celebrity. It's a celebrity, the local
drug dealer: the supplier of their
needs is gone. God, I'm not angry
at you!

People are walking away crying.
They've no hope. Someone's
standing by picking up the fragments of
their broken dreams. A mother's plea
begs her Creator for a reasonable
answer in the overcrowded drug ward
with so many victims searching for hope.
God, I'm not angry at you!

Politicians, activists, ministers, governor,
and mayor stopping by offering their
condolences as if their words have been
rehearsed over-and-over again. Their
sincerity doesn't seem real. Where
were they when the struggles began in
the streets? Were they hiding behind
Halloween masks only exposing
themselves when it was politically
expedient to win votes? God, I'm
not angry at you!

Now, the war is beginning and
the enemies are being annihilated
like the force of an atomic bomb,
signaling an end to the demonic
spirits taking over our community
and children. God, I'm not angry
at you!

I'm resting and recovering my strength. The battles are being fought from dawn to dusk with only a short break for prayer and giving thanks for Your divine intervention. God, I'm not angry at you!

THIS IS YOUR LIFE!

If somehow you could be frozen in
time, but were conscious of everything
around you without feeling pain, this is
what you'll probably hear.

Your Mother: I knew he stole the last
cookie from the cookie jar. He was
never any good at telling the truth. He
was just like his father.

Your Father: Why wasn't he like his
brother: hardworking, honest, and
conscientious? Looking on the bright
side, he was a lush like me. Boy,
could he put a few away!

Your Brother: I'm glad he's gone. Now,
I can have my room back with some
peace of mind. He dominated me, and
I didn't have the guts to tell him.

Your Sister: I'm going to hell for
covering up his lies. His girlfriends
used to call, and I'd lie saying he wasn't
home. He despised them: "no class," he
sarcastically growled! Well, he should
talk. He used to burp loudly during
dinner when they were invited.

Your Teacher: He wasn't studious. I
used to inflate his grades. Have you
heard of political correctness? What
I did was teacher correctness. Build up
students' self-esteem, and they'll
become great in life.

Your Best Friend: He'd borrow money
and would never pay me back. He was
cheaper than dirt. Thank goodness,
he's gone. Now, I can keep my money.

Your Minister: He wasn't fooling me,
and I knew he wasn't listening to
my sermons. He'd be winking at my
daughter and eyeing her cleavage.

Your Doctor: I told him he didn't have
much time to live, but he took me
seriously. It was April Fools Day!
People don't have a sense of humor like
they used to in the old days.

Your Lawyer: He was going to sue me,
but he passed away. I think the new
political correctness term is frozen in
time! I was a nervous wreck. Now, I
can keep my money. I guess God
works in mysterious ways!

Your Accountant: Yeah, I used to play
with the numbers, pretending he didn't
owe the IRS. He didn't know any
better because he trusted me. If he had
lived, I'd be ruined for life. How do
you pronounce j-a-i-l?

Your Employer: I used to tell him he
was one of my greatest employees. This
is the age of feel good therapy, you know.
Tell people they're the best, and they'll
believe it. I was going to fire him, but
his passing did the work for me.

Your Family Mortician: What did he do
to himself? The pathologist didn't sew
him up after his autopsy. His liver,
stomach, and pancreas were damaged
from all that damn drinking!

Why don't people take better care of
themselves? If there are any
perks in this profession, I'll never
worry about layoffs, underemployment,
or unemployment. Most of all, I'll never
see the same person twice, there's
always room for one more, and people
are dying to get in!

LIFE'S PLAYFUL VIGNETTES

Life's No Game

You Live!
You Learn!
You Die!
Boom! That's it.

Life's Too Short

Life's too short. I haven't
lived long enough. I've
much to do. The clock
has stopped. Won't you
rewind it?

Life's A Movie Production

Quiet, life! Let's move on.
Where's the camera?
"Broken," you say. Will
you call -- action?

Life's Nothing But Dust

Life's nothing but dust. Sand, grit:
coarse, fine, whatever. Call it what
you want, but I had no choice. My
nostrils were filled with holy air! Now,
I'm returning home -- back to dust!

Life's A Joke

Eighty years old with once
pearly whites. You're trying to
tell me something? (The roof
of your mouth is sore, and you're
gumming, too. You wished you
kissed that special girl on that
special day.) Where's she now?
In the next room? I hear her laughing,
hysterically!

Life's Running Scared

Life, why are you running
scared? You're sweating
bullets! Calm down,
breathe slowly, and listen
to the sound of the wind.
Why are you running
now? It's only the wind!

Life's A Jack-In-The-Box

Hello, my name is Jack. I'm
neatly tied, a handsome
display of sorts. Won't you
untie me? I promise I'll be
good. So, you've discovered
my secret: smile!

Life's A Card Game

Your deal. Did you cut?
(I wonder if I'll receive the
ace of life.) Life, don't
give me a raw deal: let it be
long, healthy, and prosperous.
Oh no, you dealt me the joker...
and he's laughing!

GENERATION X

The label, Generation X, which the media has given you, isn't of your own choosing. For that fact, every generation has been labeled. It isn't the label that counts, but what your generation intends to contribute to society with your time, talents, and volunteerism.

Your generation benefited academically and socially from your predecessors, the baby boomers. Doors were opened, providing for your grand entrance, and you took advantage of those opportunities. You worked, played, and loved hard, too.

Unfortunately, you were in the midst of social changes in a what-do-you-do-now! Attitudes had to be redefined with the right delicate balance in an environment of political correctness.

Now, you're gradually entering another phase of your life. Anticipating the freshness of a new millennium, your preparation is making you wiser and stronger: hopefully, in a period of prosperity, happiness, justice, and peace!

WHY WON'T SOCIETY LEAVE OTHERS ALONE?

Just because some people are different doesn't mean they're worthless. I believe in live and let live. I've enough crosses to carry without worrying about someone else's burdens. However, I realize some people won't let you in their lives unless you're invited, a standard invitation.

Let's stay out of our neighbors' bedrooms. The government invades our privacy a little too much. We don't need a repeat performance. Our personal lives aren't a grand theater production!

I'm the first to admit, we don't live in a perfect society. Moreover, we could make our society a little more tolerable, if we weren't so judgmental about others: even if they're gay.

WHEN A HOUSE ISN'T A HOME!

Some people live in a beautiful house with luxurious items. They've spared no expense competing with *Better Homes and Gardens*. For certain, their house is the envy of neighbors and friends.

A house can be an attraction: people driving slowly, pausing, and adoring its beauty. A home, in my opinion, is a resting place filled with love, joy, peace, and the laughter of family, extended family, or friends.

Yet, some houses are just the opposite: filled with sadness, fear, and apathy. For me, I'd rather live in a home than a house because a house isn't a home when no one cares.

BURNING DESIRE!

Sitting here on the soft beige couch,
illuminated by dimmed lights, and
punctuated by soft romantic music on
a stormy December evening, I long to
be embraced and wanted by you.

Even in the lights, your glowing, spell-
bound, brown eyes calm my fluttering
heart. The very thought of your strong,
muscular body aches to be touched,
explored, and used for my pleasure:
"take it off, take it off. I want you now!"
"Yes, my body needs it: work with me,
daddy." "Want me, need me, use me --
until you're exhausted!"

"Easy now -- the night's still young."
"Take your time." Damn it! The alarm
just went off. Oh well, it was only a
dream, anyway!

MISS STRUTTIN' HER STUFF!

Before judging me, I'm a person
regardless of race, creed, color,
or national origin. I'm the next
door neighbor, a family member,
or a friend. So, toss the stereotypes out
the window, and let's go from here!

I'm considered a fine, foxy lady by my
clients' standards: 5'11"; lovely facial
features; beautiful long, brown hair;
long legs; and a silky complexion.
I'm attending medical school during the
day, and in the evening, I'm earning
extra money paying for medical school.
I usually make two thousand dollars a
night working for an escort service in a
large metropolitan city.

My clients are the well-known pillars of
the community: people you wouldn't
suspect of using an escort service. I
adore my clients because they say I've
class, and I can be taken anywhere
within reason. My job is servicing
their needs. Who am I to judge? I eat
lavishly in the classiest restaurants.
The gentlemen tell their wives they're
going out of town on business. This
isn't unusual because their
occupations require traveling.

After our sumptuous meal and
returning to a hotel, I service them.
They want me struttin' in four inch
heels, and of course, the rest of the
evening is left up to the readers'
imagination! I've never had a
dissatisfied client because I know
them well. They've built a bond and
a trust with me. I'd never blackmail
them because they need me. The
money isn't bad. I work four evenings,
about an hour for each client, seeing
five clients. My weekends are my time.

My clients gave me that name...Miss
Struttin' Her Stuff, and the name has
been with me since. When I've saved
enough money, I'm quitting the service
and opening my medical practice.
Those fond memories I'll always cherish.
By the way, I'll be graduating from
medical school next year. I'll be struttin'
my stuff across the stage receiving my
degree. Don't you think I deserve it?

ILLEGAL AND UNWANTED

I thought America was the land of opportunity for all people and not just a few. Well, you could've fooled me. Give me your tired your poor...hogwash! I'm illegal and unwanted. Illegal because I'm not a citizen, and as far as the government is concerned, I don't possess any valuable skills.

You see, I was a waitress in my country. There was turmoil, fighting, bullets flying everywhere, anytime, and at anyone. Death surrounded me which was depressing, along with losing relatives and friends.

When there was silence that was a treat! I savored those quiet moments just catching my breath since I never knew when the soldiers would start shelling again. Lord knows, I saw enough death and destruction for a lifetime. That's why I submitted my application for political asylum. The officials rejected my requests for the fifth time. Luckily, I had a friend going to the United States. He sneaked me in illegally in the back of his truck. The immigration officers must have been distracted. They didn't check our truck. So, that's how I entered unnoticed.

Since I was willing to pay a hefty price for documents, I found work almost immediately. Believe me, I would've taken any job just to survive. I did what I had to do! My employer hired illegals, using and exploiting them.

With four of us living in a two bedroom apartment, we saved money. This was luxury compared to my homeland, one big room, and people couldn't understand that.

I remember some coworkers rolling their eyes, giving me the impression that I, along with the others, weren't wanted! Other verbal rantings were: "go home, we don't need you here!" "Why are you taking our jobs away?" "We've met our quotas, you're a day too late," laughing hysterically! That's OK, I'll be reapplying for political asylum.

Whenever I become a citizen, I'll no longer have to say to myself: illegal and unwanted!

RAINY DAY, STORMY NIGHT!

On a cool, October morning with winds blowing a large, lush pine tree in front of my perfectly manicured lawn, I'm finding myself facing my bathroom mirror and attending to my bruises for, what seems, the hundredth time from another knock-down-drag-out fight with my husband. Here again, I pretend I'm content in our relationship.

Oh, I know there has been good times. He sometimes takes me to dinner and dancing. Boy, there are some nice qualities about him. He can dance his tight buns off! Then, after our night on the town, he makes passionate and seemingly unending love. Even in my denial, I call this happy moment my rainy day!

Five children, 8-13, and ten years of a stormy marriage hasn't been a talk show tell all. I'm always commenting to my girlfriend on the phone: "people appearing on talk shows are dysfunctional, telling their personal business." "Heaven's sake, isn't anything personal and sacred anymore?"

Don't get me wrong, I love my husband and my children. Lord, I've made poor choices. Is that a sin? My husband loves his children. The children despise the way he's treating me. The younger ones angrily speak of harming him when they become older. Constantly, I'm reassuring them, it won't be necessary because God works in mysterious ways! I'd always choose fine, fast talking, well-dressed men who could charm the clothes off me. Well, my husband's a worthy candidate: fine, a charmer, and quite articulate. If only I had seen the clues while dating, I wouldn't be in this situation. There were jealous bouts, little slaps (as he called them), bitter arguments over money, and sporadic drinking binges.

I knew when I was younger, I wasn't going to marry this type of man, but...my biological time clock was winding down, and I felt so old. I was twenty three! I'm blessed in one way, he loves working. He won't let me work: "too much women's liberation," he laments! Time-and-time again, I try leaving, but I can't leave this man.

Counseling? Are you kidding? He's too macho for that stuff! He reassures me -- there's nothing wrong with him, it's me.

Another day goes by, and in a sense, I'm alone with my memories of what may happen: beatings and more beatings! Lord, give me strength to run this race!

Listening to the sound of the slowly, inserted key, I'm preparing myself. Lord, no, he's drunk again. He's angry, defiant, and this is my stormy night. He's beating me...sweet Jesus!

THE PLAYER

"Come here, you foxy, sapphire, long-legged bosom-filled lady," shouts the player. "Come to daddy and bring your best wine. Your treat?" "I've been watching you so long." "Lady, where have you been?" "Listen, I'm for real. Can't you feel me?"

"Did I hear you say money is your game?" "OK, how about making me some?" "Damn you," screams the lady! "I don't need no damn pimp." "Baby," retorts the player, "I need you."

Angrily, she's turning away knowing if she submits, she'll be losing her soul to the prince of darkness! She's thinking to herself. There's something about this man that doesn't seem right. Away from the lights, the glitter, and jolting herself back to reality, she gasps in horror. This man's my father!

THE LADIES OF THE EVENING!

The ladies of the evening are prowling
the streets, seeking victims for their
pleasure. The men are accommodating
and showering them with attention,
gifts, and pretended love!

Glittering lights, fast paced cars, noisy,
chattering pedestrians are filling the crowded
street, mingling with the famous and
infamous who are seeking their own
attention and stardom for even a moment.

Seedy hotels and motels extending a
welcome to the ladies with a posted
sign: ROOMS FOR RENT! Approaching
these dim lit corridors sometimes
reluctantly and willingly are their
evening trade, and after servicing,
lamenting, "no more trade tonight!"

The ladies of the evening justify their
actions by explaining away their deeds
to friends or anyone who'll listen:
"it's good money, pays the rent, and
doctor's bill!"

"Condoms anyone," a lady asks?
"We've different colors and different
flavors. This is high tech, now!"
Quickly finishing their sexual conquests,
they go their separate ways in a city
without a name!

LIVING ON THE EDGE!

Personally, I like living on the edge…
it's exciting, thrilling, and deadly. I
think it's the deadly part I enjoy, giving
me a natural high.

I'm not a drinker, smoker, or drug
user. My friends and I go drag racing
on the main strip, not wearing any
seat belts. To us, they're too
restricting. We also enjoy racing at
top notch speeds trying to elude the
police. Don't you get it? We like
living on the edge!

When it comes to sex, we don't use
condoms: too unnatural and real
men don't need them. Anyway, the
women we meet don't enjoy them.
Don't you get it? We like living on
the edge!

I never can understand those nine-to-
five snobbish, boardroom types who
live life too conservatively. They act
as if they're afraid of breathing. For
us, we want to enjoy life: live it,
savor its bitter fruits. What generation
didn't break any rules? Tell me one,

and I'll wager you're lying. Even those
so-called 1950's "good girls" got
pregnant, but the community kept it
a secret. Yeah, there was plenty of
sex in the back seats of those cars,
and they weren't man and wife, either.
Don't you get it? We like living on
the edge!

Now, it's our time to be free spirited,
good natured, and hearty. Our
friends will continue living on the edge
until we, one day, fall off that cliff of
life. Don't you get it? We like living
on the edge!

THE DEMONS WITHIN

Some of us have hidden demons we dare not expose. We live, work, study, and play with our demons while going about our daily routines. It's amazing some of us are in control. We're masters of deception!

What are some of these demons? Prejudice; pride; fear; greed; hypocrisy; lust; self-hatred; anger; dishonesty; jealousy; impatience; procrastination; vindictiveness; intemperance; disobedience; spiritual blindness; and covetousness.

In my opinion, the only way these demons can be exorcised is by faith, humility, and prayer. Unfortunately for some, these anomalies will always be a part of their survival kit!

THE PRISONER OF MY SOUL

Scattered on my dresser are an assortment of pills ranging from aspirin to mind altering drugs. I've been using drugs since twelve when friends introduced me to them. I'm now twenty-one and a mess! I've tried stopping, but I keep returning to those comforting pills. Yes, I've been to clinics and anonymous meetings but nothing works. Therapists and psychiatrists haven't helped.

My father was a drug user and an alcoholic. My mother wasn't any help because she was dysfunctional. He whipped her butt breakfast, lunch, and dinner for the smallest infraction. Believe me, she had her own hell! My sister was just two. She doesn't remember anything. I'm a prisoner and my soul is tormented!

Religion? I've tried that, too. It works for awhile, but I refuse to submit to any religious denomination or doctrine. I'm my own temple. It's not that I don't believe in God, but when I want to do right, something or someone comes in between.

Since attending the local community college, I've been around negative peers. They drink, smoke, and use drugs. Thank goodness, I don't smoke or drink. If I did, I'd probably be dead! I coach myself saying I can quit. I just need a little will power. Each night before going to bed, I look at those pills, turn away, but something seems to draw me to them as if they're speaking: "take me; no, take me!" I've tried knocking them off my dresser, but I become tired stepping over bottles, eventually picking them up, placing them on the dresser, and looking at them.

Morning comes, the sun's blazing in my window, and I feel like a zombie. Another day of living with my demons. I know I've to get ready for work, but dragging myself out of bed is a chore. Let's see, feet first or head first. Ouch! Oh, my aching head. Can this be real?
Getting my bearings, I slowly lift myself off the floor, right foot first for balance and then the left. Now, I'm sitting on the edge of the bed

with my hands tightly gripped. I'm afraid of moving for fear of falling off again.

A half hour passes; it seems almost four hours. I've not moved from the bed: frozen in time. Looking around my cluttered, unkept sterile-like white room, I search for more pills. There are some lying on the carpeted floor near my feet. I'm too sore to bend over and get them, but I need my friends:
they love me, make me feel secure, and painless.

My mind is racing and my conscience is tinkering on exploding. I feel as if I'm in a prison. Am I hallucinating? I see burly correction officers coming for me with their assortment of dangling keys unlocking my tormented soul.

No, it's my imagination. Somehow, my prison is unlocked, and it's deadly. I wonder when this life will be over. I can't bear the torment any longer. God, help me!

DEADLY SILENCE!

That fresh spring-like day in April with the chirping birds perched on a large tree in front of my apartment gave me reason to get up and get out: that extra push I needed to face the day. If I knew what was to be expected, I'd have stayed home, read a good book, or just lounged around doing absolutely nothing. There wasn't anything in my wildest dreams that would've predicted what was to take place.

I ate a hurried breakfast: cereal, toasted bagel with a smear of cream cheese, and gulped my orange juice and coffee down. Then, I took a quick shower, got dressed, and left my apartment around 9:30 a.m. to run errands.

My apartment is located near a long, wide alley where cars aren't welcomed, let alone, pedestrians. The alley's notoriously dangerous and many lives have been lost -- being in the wrong place -- at the wrong time! Since I'm familiar with the area, I sprint because the masked killer(s) would hide behind trash dumpsters and on top of buildings waiting to pounce on innocent victims, killing them depending upon the day's horoscope predictions. I can't figure out why April 15 is one of the bloodiest days in the alley of the dead! The predators would strike in the day and in the night by throwing their victims off guard.

Usually, before leaving my apartment, I'd read my horoscope -- as I was born on April 15. Somehow, getting sidetracked that morning, I forgot to check. Anyway, turning the corner, I noticed what seemed to be a person covered with blood-soaked rags and newspapers, lying near a large, brown closed trash container.

Removing the tainted evidence, gasping in horror, and silently uttering: [this man's famous, a well respected journalist], I began rearranging the rags on his face. Looking toward the well lit roof, I noticed a tall, thin man dressed in black, also wearing a black mask, and staring at me. I suddenly froze -- afraid of running. Jumping from the second story roof like a well conditioned athlete, he whispered: "keep your mouth shut, or you'll be the next victim." "I know where you live. Now, do your errands!"

Finding the courage and lifting my cement-like feet, I nervously repeated over-and-over again: feet, don't fail me now. I ran, ran, and ran. Somehow, finding myself in front of a beautiful gothic church, I went in, knelt, and prayed with sweat running like buckets of water.

Suddenly, a cold chill was racing through my body as I frighteningly looked over my left shoulder. Here was this man in black, hesitating for a moment. Then, he entered the confessional, I guess, to repent of his crime in the alley. While trembling like an aftershock of an earthquake, it dawned on me, he wasn't the confessor, but the...!

THE UNATTAINABLE

I watch you strut with your broad
shoulders and strong, chiseled arms
bulging through your open shirt. I
imagine you're planting a kiss
on my blushing cheeks as I anticipate
your soft, manly lips.

I eye you from a distance and long to
run into your waiting arms to be held
so closely: begging you to whisper --
just anything in my ear -- as long as
your breath touches my skin.

Your manly scent makes me want
to explode inside. A sniff of you is
all I need to feel womanly. I know
you're unattainable because you
belong to another, but I need the
reassurance I'll always be in
your heart.

Walking away from me, I shutter to
think one day I may never see you
again. We'll go our separate ways,
but I can dream of what I couldn't
have, the unattainable!

Denise Michelle Phillips

1999 AND COUNTING

Lights, camera, action! It'll be that time
again, another new year with the
anticipation of boisterous merrymaking
from north to south and from east to
west, disregarding time or temperature!

Hopes, dreams, and new loves: the
beginning of new wishes, challenges,
and good intentions. Kisses blown at
unsuspecting strangers, handshakes
extending to the inebriated, catching them
off-balanced, and laughter resounding
throughout the "Times Squares" of
America and beyond.

Who'll be the lucky recipients of
this holiday ranting with spectators
embracing their friends, family, or
lovers on this momentous celebration?

Let's fast forward. So, the countdown
begins: 5, 4, 3, 2, 1...! The 1999 ball's
descending; people in churches for new
year's watch; champagne corks popping
everywhere; firecrackers going off; and
people in clubs dancing their last dance
in this decade. Their loves, hates, and fears
of yesterday are forever vanished in time
as no year repeats itself. The moving
clock ticks, and it can't wait for
anyone to rewind it or steal time. One
day, the last chime will sound, never
to be heard again, silencing the end of
the age!